AUSTRIAN TEXTILES

The object of this series is to present a Survey of World Textiles, each volume dealing with a separate country. The undermentioned are published or in course of preparation.

Other volumes are to follow and will be announced from time to time

AUSTRIAN TEXTILES

by

DR. FRITZ STELLWAG-CARION

F. LEWIS, PUBLISHERS, LTD.
LEIGH-ON-SEA

PRINTED IN THE NETHERLANDS

First published 1960

Printed by Meyer of Wormerveer
Bound by A. W. Bain & Co, Ltd., London

Introduction

AUSTRIA, renowned the world over as an ideal tourist country with magnificent scenery and as the home of the Viennese waltz, operettas and 'savoir vivre', could be equally renowned for the products of her textile industry. As compared with other countries, the 70,000 workers employed in the textile industry may not seem a great number, yet there is hardly a textile article which is not produced in Austria. Annual exports have reached 30 million pounds sterling representing one-fourth of the total production.

Most widely known are, perhaps, the products of the Vorarlberg embroidery industry. Switzerland and Austria are the world's leading exporting countries in this particular field, competing with each other as to the quality and beauty of their products. The cotton industry is, however, the largest textile branch in Austria and its coloured woven and printed cottons and spun-rayon fabrics have become very popular all over the world.

As to wool fabrics, Austria is especially known for worsteds, in particular for her water-proofed 'Loden' cloth, used mainly for coatings and ideal for hunting, shooting or other outdoor activities.

The silk industry is internationally known for its rich jacquard woven fabrics for afternoon and evening wear. Tie materials and typically Austrian costumes are also being exported in large quantities.

Apart from being the Capital city of Austria, Vienna is the centre of the knitting industry, its products ranging from weave-knit dresses to ski-ing jackets, sports socks and fancy gloves.

The illustrations in this book are but a small sample of the wide variety and the high quality of Austrian textiles.

I should like to express here my particular gratitude to Dr. G. Bruckmann and Miss M. Stejskal, as well as to the Association of the Vorarlberg Embroidery Industries and to all participating firms for their invaluable assistance in making possible this volume. May it help to win new friends for Austria, the land and its products.

DR. FRITZ STELLWAG-CARION

page seven

Descriptive Notes
on the Illustrations

Figure 1   Coloured woven fabrics for sports-shirts, rayon or cotton, crease-resistant or no-iron finish. From F. M. Hämmerle, Dornbirn.

Figure 2   From F. M. Hämmerle, Dornbirn, producers of fine cotton poplins for pyjamas. In a variety of designs and colourings. Sanforised.

Figures 3 and 4   Woven fashionable dress-materials in fine cottons. Available in crease-resistant or no-iron finish. Courtesy of F. M. Hämmerle, Dornbirn.

Figure 5   Cotton flannel blanket with traditional rose design in Jacquard weave. From Herrburger & Rhomberg, Dornbirn, Innsbruck and Vienna.

Figure 6   Bedding printed with floral stripes, woven of pure cotton, for pillows and feather beds. From Herrburger & Rhomberg, Dornbirn, Innsbruck and Vienna.

Figure 7   Garden table-cloth in modern design and reversible weave. It can be used on either side and is woven of double cotton yarns. From Herrburger & Rhomberg, Dornbirn, Innsbruck and Vienna.

Figure 8 Typical Austrian garden table-cloth. Check design with staggered clover leaves woven in. Weave: Alternately warp and weft satin. Material: pure cotton. From Herrburger & Rhomberg, Dornbirn, Innsbruck and Vienna.

Figures 9 *and* 10 Sports-shirtings of various designs and colours, made from 100% cotton with fancy yarns and printed in a variety of patterns. From Pottendorfer Spinnerei & Felixdorfer Weberei A.G., Vienna.

Figure 11 '*Elfi*': Pure cotton yarn, crease-resistant finish with cross-borders and pastel coloured stripes; the ideal material for light summer dress wear. From Martin Stapf, Imst/Tyrol.

Figure 12 '*Sibylle*': a new fashionable Jacquard woven textile fabric with embroidery effects. Pure cotton yarn, crease-resistant finish. From Martin Stapf, Imst/Tyrol.

Figure 13 '*Jacqueline*': an ultra-modern hand-print upon a pure wool natural tissue; it can be used for skirts, blouses and dressing-gowns. From Martin Stapf, Imst/Tyrol.

Figure 14 '*Zeelandia*': a brocade-like and multi-purposed fabric with striped design. Pure cotton yarn. From Martin Stapf, Imst/Tyrol.

Figure 15 '*Firn*': Geniune Tyrolian braids, for generations a speciality of Martin Stapf, Imst/Tyrol. Some of the patterns are centuries old, some in ultra-modern designs. Used for skirts, blouses, aprons, parkas, as well as in the shoe and slipper industry, but also as a furnishing fabric.

Figures 16 *and* 17   '*Eden Skirts*': smart, washable summer-skirts (Do it Yourself), to be made in a short time without special knowledge of sewing. An ideal and inexpensive garment for warm days made of first-class crease-resisting materials, available in many patterns and colours. From Theresienthaler Baumwollspinnerei und Weberei, A.G., Vienna.

Figure 18   '*Montana*', a Sunfrock from Franz M. Rhomberg, Dornbirn.

Figure 19   '*Veronika*': these delightful Tyrolian dresses come from Franz M. Rhomberg, Dornbirn.

Figure 20   (Top) '*Bettina*'—doubled yarn spun rayon woven in true tartans. Wool finish, crease-resisting. (Centre) '*Yvo-Broche*'—spun rayon fabric with different dobby-effects in rural designs. Bright colours and melange yarns make this a very suitable fabric for childrens' wear and the teenager. (Bottom) Spun rayon fabric with a woolly handle. Mainly styled in small plaids particularly suitable for school-girl dresses and pleated skirts; crease resisting. From Getzner, Mutter & Cie., Bludenz.

Figures 21 *and* 22   Two curtain fabrics from J. M. Fussenegger, Dornbirn (Bleachers, Dyers, Printers, Finishers and Weavers). All the fancy designs are printed with guaranteed fast colours (Indanthren).

Figure 23   Baby Bibs, small orange juice bibs, pure chenille multi-coloured with terry bindings. From Johann Garber & Sohn, Vienna.

Figure 24   Baby Bibs and pinafore Bibs, jacquard woven with nursery rhymes, terry with chenille. From Johann Garber & Sohn, Vienna.

Figure 25 'Peter'—a hooded cape, handwoven terry towelling with multi-coloured chenille border. From Johann Garber & Sohn, Vienna.

Figure 26 Terry cloths in a range of varying patterns. From Schlesische Leinen-und Damastweberei Nachf. E. Machold K.G., Götzis.

Figure 27 Damask table cloth. From Schlesische Leinen-und Damastweberei Nachf. E. Machold K.G., Götzis.

Figure 28 'Tirol', table cloth with matching napkins, half linen in different colours. From Vonwiller & Co., Haslach.

Figure 29 'Ischil', table cloth with matching napkins, half linen and available in different colours. From Vonwiller & Co., Haslach.

Figure 30 'Cocktail', Tea-cloth in pure linen, 23 ½ inches square. Colours: pink, red and lilac. From Vonwiller & Co., Haslach.

Figure 31 'Cocktail', pure linen tea-cloth, 23 ½ inches square and available in green, red or lilac. From Vonwiller & Co., Haslach.

Figure 32 Worsteds and woollens for ladies and gentlemens' wear, woven by Wiener Kleiderstoff-und Tuchfabrik Ges.m.b.H., Vienna, of worsted and woollen yarns spun by A.G. der Vöslauer Kammgarnfabrik, Bad Vöslau.

Figures 33 *and* 34 Geniune Tyrolean Himalaya Loden cloth, waterproofed. 70% pure wool, 30% mohair. From Vereinigte Tuchfabriken Baur-Foradori, Innsbruck.

Figure 35   Geniune Tyrolean Loden cloth, waterproofed, 70% pure wool, 30% mohair. From Vereinigte Tuchfabriken Baur-Foradori, Innsbruck.

Figures 36 and 37   An assortment of products from Franz Pischl, Telfs/Tyrol, well known for his fine Loden cloths, as well as for fashionable carded woollen cloth, i.e., flannels, gabardines and suitings for both ladies and gentlemen, in pure wool.

Figure 38   These high-class fancy worsteds are typical of the cloth made by Inzersdorfer Weberei Brüder Selinko, Vienna. This firm manufactures worsted flannels, gabardine, serge, hopsack, etc., and high grade fancy suitings; and plain and fancy dress goods in worsteds for ladies wear.

Figure 39   A rich collection of blankets in bright colours and modern patterns, also for babies, as well as blankets of pure camel hair and special blankets for hospitals and similar institutions. From Vereinigte Tuch-und Deckenfabriken Sannwald & Co., Bregenz.

Figure 40   Plaids of pure wool and finest mohair in bright colours and contemporary patterns. From Vereinigte Tuch-und Deckenfabriken Sannwald & Co., Bregenz.

Figure 41   Spool-Axminster, '*Rio*' quality in '*Aras*' design. This quality is made in rugs in a wide choice of modern and Oriental designs and is in vogue on account of its bright and contemporary colours. The Oriental designs are especially adapted to these rug sizes, whereas the modern designs are remarkable for their ample colour-assortment. From A.G. der Teppich-und Möbelstoff-Fabriken, vorm Philipp Haas & Söhne, Vienna.

Figures 42, 43 and 44   Gripper-Axminster '*Astoria*' range. This quality is made in a variety of the finest and best selling Oriental designs, in a number of standard colours, and in all Continental carpet sizes. Figure 42. Design '*Sultan*'. Figure 43. Design '*Bathiary*'. Figure 44. Design '*Karadja*'. From A. G. der Teppich-und Möbelstoff-Fabriken, vorm. Philipp Haas & Söhne, Vienna.

Figure 45   Coir-carpet in red, black, white and grey. Sizes: 175 × 250 cm and 200 × 300 cm. From Erste Österreichische Mechanische Kokosteppich-und Mattenfabrik Karl Eybl, Krems-Stein. Producers of coir mattings and carpets and sisal mattings.

Figures 46 *and* 47   Favourite designs of umbrella cloths produced in many fashionable colours (stripes, checks or ombré), from the silk weaving Mill of J. Adensamer & Cie., Vienna. Producers of linings (plain, stripes, checks and satin) and umbrella cloths (a world-wide export material). The firm also manufacture all kinds of silk and velvet ribbons.

Figure 48   This is a representative illustration of the productions of A. Flemmich's Söhne, Vienna. They produce Silks for National costumes, pure silk kerchiefs and scarves of traditional design – all these in a great variety of qualities, patterns and colours. This firm also produce Ecclessiastical furnishings.

Figure 49   Pure silk kerchiefs of the Austrian type with knotted fringes, the striped pattern slightly resembling the 'Biedermeier' period. From A. Flemmich's Söhne, Vienna.

Figure 50   '*Libussa*' a Jacquard weave in an interesting matelassé design for evening dresses. Material: rayon/spun rayon. From Gebrüder Schiel A.G., Vienna.

Figure 51   Printed six-colour Trevira-Twill for the finest ladies summer dresses. Material: 100% polyester. From Gebrüder Schiel A.G., Vienna.

Figure 52   Tie materials in acetate organzine, Bemberg, Polyester and pure silk. Classic and modern designs in fashionable colours. From Wiener Seidenweberei Alfred Fiala, Vienna.

Figure 53   Brocade for afternoon and evening wear in Bemberg, acetate organzine, combined perlon and wool material. Plastic embroidery effects and small relief-like motives emphasize the individual note of this collection. From Wiener Seidenweberei Alfred Fiala, Vienna.

Figure 54   Tie materials, a leading export article of the Wiener-Neustadter Seidenindustrie Kober & Co., Wien.

Figure 55   A selection of brocades from Wiener-Neustadter Seidenindustrie Kober & Co., Wien. Besides the traditional materials, Rhodie-acetate, Viscose, Lurex and Crylor are being used more and more, to achieve further variations.

Figure 56   Lurex-brocade, a pleasant design for evening and cocktail dresses. Jacquard weave, a typical Austrian fashion for national costume. From Heinrich Löri, Vienna.

Figure 57   (Left) Relief brocade in a shrunk finish based on Rhovyl, for skirts and dresses. Crease resistant and exceptionally hardwearing. (Right) A Jacquard weave in Bemberg wool mixture, very popular for skirts and sportswear. From Heinrich Löri, Vienna.

Figure 58   Jacquard Matelassé, on rayon warp with rayon and cotton weft, pastel shades and crease resisting finish. Available in many different designs. From Brüder Steiner, Vienna.

Figures 59 *and* 60   Jacquard brocades, on rayon warp with rayon and Lurex filling. From Brüder Steiner, Vienna.

Figures 61, 62, 63, *and* 64   Curtains, curtain nets, table covers and table sets in various forms and sizes, from M. Faber & Co. Wien. Messrs: Faber are manufacturers of all kinds of woven laces, both in cotton and synthetic fibres.

Figures 65 *to* 73 Products of the Vorarlberg Embroidery Industry. (Photo's supplied by Verband der Vorarlberger Stickerei-Industrie in Dornbirn.) Figure 65. Embroidered blouse-front, muslin, 53 inches, no-iron finish. Figure 66. Embroidered cambric-edgings, white/white. Figure 67. 53 inch Silk-organza, with an embroidered allover design. Silk or Lurex. Figure 68. Embroidered nylon-edging. Figure 69. Embroidered cambric edging. Figure 70. Embroidered flouncing, tone on tone on cotton crepe. Figure 71. Embroidered nylon-edging, 2-colour embroidery on a sheer fabric. Figure 72. Guipure allover, cotton, white, 36 inches. Figure 73. Embroidered silk-taffeta with appliqued guipure-edge, 48 inches.

Figure 74 '*Efeu*' a dress in mohair-wool jersey. Empire silhouette with raised waistline, fashion belted in the back. In four colours. From Jerlaine Benger & Co., Vienna.

Figure 75 '*Aachensee*', an attractive cocktail dress in black with a big collar and rose, in the new Jerlaine fabric 'Jovienne', 100% stretch nylon, silk-like appearance, washable, no-iron. From Jerlaine Benger & Co., Vienna.

Figure 76 Fashionable knitted dress, raised pattern design. Available in lovely light pastel colourings. From P. M. Glaser, Vienna.

Figure 77 This suit in Jacquard weave knit comes from Dobyhal & Co., Vienna. The dress (with belt) showing the Empire line.

Figure 78 '*Marion*', suit made of jersey jacquard weave-knit. 100% virgin wool. From Siegfried Elias, Vienna.

Figure 79 Here is an elegant ensemble comprising a Shopping or occasional jacket, Miramare sweater and Ascot skirt. From 'Hummer' Wiener Mode, Vienna.

Figures 80 *and* 81   Jackets and skirts from 'Hummer', Wiener Mode, Vienna.

Figure 82   '*Inge*', in boutique-style, teenage model made of pure wool weave-knit, the small gold embroidered pocket being the only ornament of the jacket. From 'Madelaine', Franz Mäser, Dornbirn.

Figure 83   '*Roxy*', two-piece ensemble of pure wool weave-knit, the white edging contrasting with the blue of this model. The broad front belt, Empire line, is buttoned upon the dress. From 'Madelaine', Franz Mäser, Dornbirn.

Figure 84   Fully fashioned pullover with three-quarter sleeves, a fancy pastel striped design with a shirt collar. From 'Wispo', Pschikal & Co., Vienna.

Figure 85   '*World Champion*', a special sports pullover, the material containing water-resisting wool and rubber threads, rendering the best possible service for sportswear. From 'Wispo', Pschikal & Co., Vienna.

Figure 86   An extravagant bathing-suit. The material is plain coloured lastex-satin, the pleated front imparting that 'dressy' look and a soft feminine line. From 'Wispo', Pschikal & Co., Vienna.

Figure 87   Vari-coloured coarse-knit sweater from Franz Kugler, Vienna.

Figure 88   '*Five O'Clock*'—a jumper suit in weave-knit and embroidery. For cocktail, theatre and dinner parties. From 'Sport Nouvelle', S. Katz & Co., Vienna.

Figure 89 *'Cruise'*–dress in white/navy stripe. This delightful ensemble has a matching jacket in fine quality weave-knit and an exciting pillar-box red leather belt. From 'Sport Nouvelle', S. Katz & Co., Vienna.

Figure 90 *'Sabrina'*, jacket in pure merino wool with wide attractive knitted braid edging. From Benedikt Mäser, Dornbirn.

Figure 91 *Iris/Dolfi* cardigan, all lace macramé, three quarter sleeves. From Steffi Zambra, Vienna.

Figure 92 *'Florenz'*, jumper suit, an attractive dress worked in macramé. From Steffi Zambra, Vienna.

Figure 93 *Iris II/Schlange*, an all macramé embroidered cardigan. From Steffi Zambra, Vienna.

Figure 94 *'Caprice'*, knitted two-piece in pure wool. From 'Corona Vienna', Günther Tassul & Co., Vienna.

Figure 95 *'Effie'*, jumper with macramé embroidery in pure wool. From 'Corona Vienna', Günther Tassul & Co., Vienna.

Figure 96 Club jacket with Austrian Coat-of-Arms and pleated skirt. From Leopold Hoffmann, Vienna.

Figure 97 Heavy knitted cardigan with large collar in combination with a pair of trousers in plain weave-knit. From Leopold Hoffmann, Vienna.

Figure 98 Jacket of pure wool weave-knit combined with leather, and a pair of trousers in the same material. From Leopold Hoffmann, Vienna.

Figure 99 (Left) A *'Hellas-Volant'*, glove, in top grade merino. Washable English leather has been used for the hand-sewn palm. (Centre) A classic honeycomb in high bulk orlon. (Right) A fine knitted glove with an original leather trimming. From 'Hellas', Jirges & Co., Vienna.

ILLUSTRATIONS

FIG. I FROM F. M. HÄMMERLE, DORNBIRN

FIG. 2. FROM F. M. HÄMMERLE, DORNBIRN

FIG. 3. FROM F. M. HÄMMERLE, DORNBIRN

FIG. 4. FROM F. M. HÄMMERLE, DORNBIRN

FIG. 5. FROM HERRBURGER & RHOMBERG, INNSBRUCK

FIG. 6. FROM HERRBURGER & RHOMBERG, INNSBRUCK

FIG. 7. FROM HERRBURGER & RHOMBERG, INNSBRUCK

FIG. 8. FROM HERRBURGER & RHOMBERG, INNSBRUCK

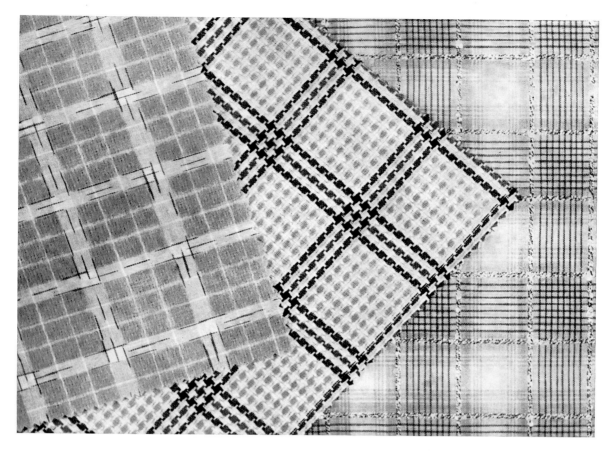

FIG. 9. FROM POTTENDORFER SPINNEREI UND FELIXDORFER WEBEREI A.G., WIEN

FIG. 10. FROM POTTENDORFER SPINNEREI UND FELIXDORFER WEBEREI A.G., WIEN

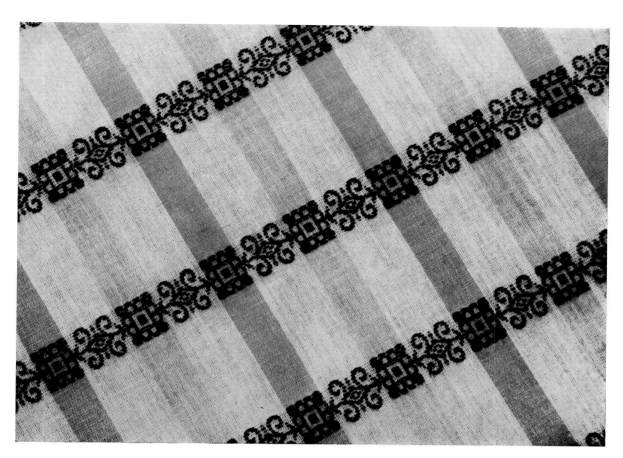

FIG. II. FROM MARTIN STAPF, IMST/TYROL

FIG. 12. FROM MARTIN STAPF, IMST/TYROL

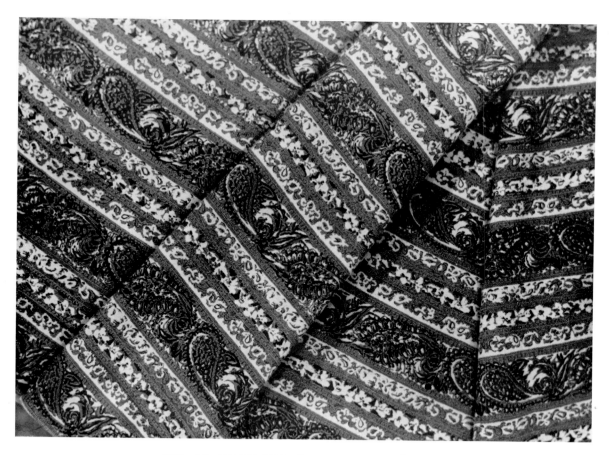

FIG. 13. FROM MARTIN STAPF, IMST/TYROL

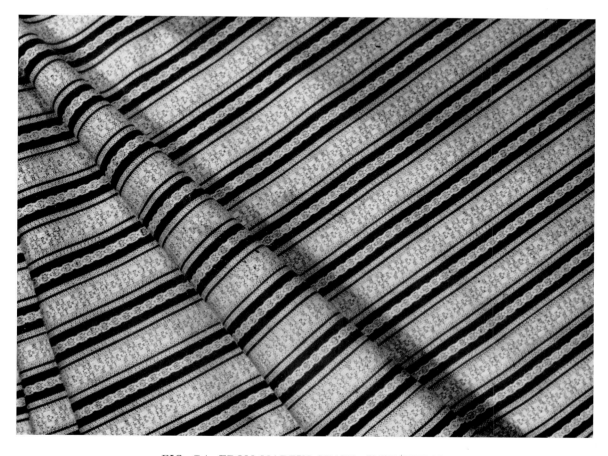

FIG. 14. FROM MARTIN STAPF, IMST/TYROL

FIG. 15. FROM MARTIN STAPF, IMST/TYROL

FIG. 16 & 17. FROM THERESIENTHALER BAUMWOLLSPINNEREI UND WEBEREI A.G., WIEN

FIG. 18. FROM FRANZ M. RHOMBERG,
DORNBIRN

FIG. 19. FROM FRANZ M. RHOMBERG, DORNBIRN

FIG. 20. FROM GETZNER, MUTTER & CIE., BLUDENZ

FIG. 21. FROM J. M. FUSSENEGGER, DORNBIRN

FIG. 22. FROM J. M. FUSSENEGGER, DORNBIRN

FIG. 23. FROM JOHANN GARBER & SÖHN, WIEN

FIG. 24. FROM JOHANN GARBER & SÖHN, WIEN

FIG. 25. FROM JOHANN GARBER & SÖHN, WIEN

FIG. 26. FROM SCHLESISCHE LEINEN UND DAMASTWEBEREI NACHF. E. MACHOLD
K.G., GÖTZIS

FIG. 27. FROM SCHLESISCHE LEINEN UND DAMASTWEBEREI NACHF.
E. MACHOLD K.G., GÖTZIS

FIG. 28. FROM VONWILLER & CO., HASLACH

FIG. 29. FROM VONWILLER & CO., HASLACH

FIG. 30. FROM VONWILLER & CO., HASLACH

FIG. 31 FROM VONWILLER & CO., HASLACH

FIG. 32. FROM WIENER KLEIDERSTOFF UND TUCHFABRIK GES.M.B.H., WIEN

FIG. 33. FROM VEREINIGTE TUCHFABRIKEN BAUR-FORADORI, INNSBRUCK

FIG. 34. FROM VEREINIGTE TUCHFABRIKEN BAUR-FORADORI, INNSBRUCK

FIG. 35. FROM VEREINIGTE TUCHFABRIKEN BAUR-FORADORI, INNSBRUCK

FIG. 36. FROM LODEN UND SCHAFWOLLWARENFABRIK FRANZ PISCHL, TELFS

FIG. 37. FROM LODEN UND SCHAFWOLLWARENFABRIK FRANZ PISCHL, TELFS

FIG. 38. FROM INZERSDORFER WEBEREI BRÜDER SELINKO, WIEN

FIG. 39. FROM VEREINIGTE TUCH UND DECKENFABRIKEN
SANNWALD & CO., BREGENZ

FIG. 40. FROM VEREINIGTE TUCH UND DECKENFABRIKEN
SANNWALD & CO., BREGENZ

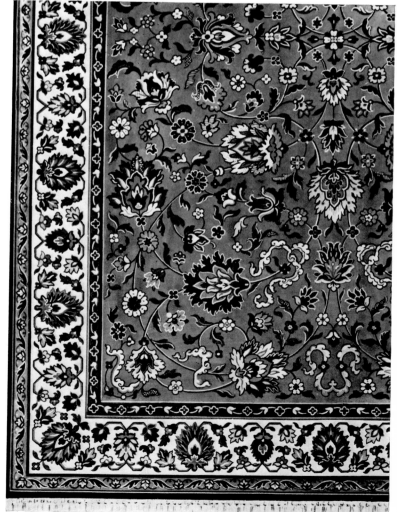

OM 42. FROM A.G. DER TEPPICH UND MÖBELSTOF-
FABRIKEN VORM PHILIPP HAAS & SÖHNE, WIEN

FIG. 43. FROM A.G. DER TEPPICH UND MÖBELSTOF-
FABRIKEN VORM PHILIPP HAAS & SÖHNE, WIEN

FIG. 44. FROM A.G. DER TEPPICH UND MÖBELSTOFFABRIKEN VORM PHILIPP HAAS &
SÖHNE, WIEN

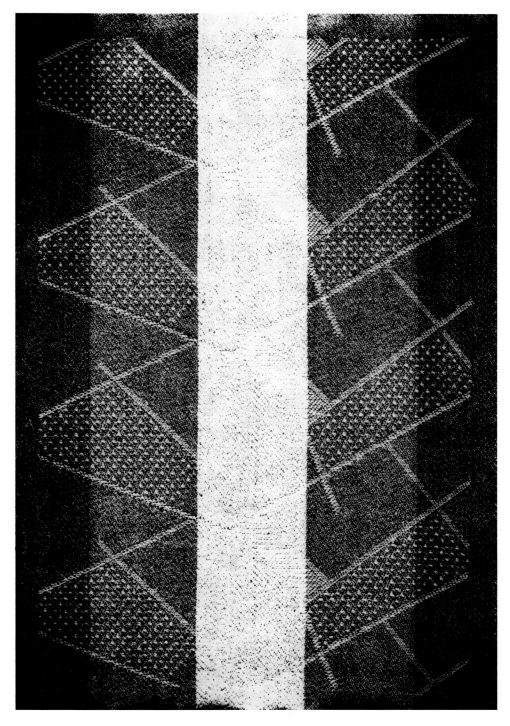

FIG. 45. FROM ERSTE ÖSTERREICHISCHE MECHANISCHE KOKOSTEPPICH
UND MATTENFABRIK KARL EYBL, KREMS-STEIN

FIG. 46. FROM J. ADENSAMER & CIE., WIEN

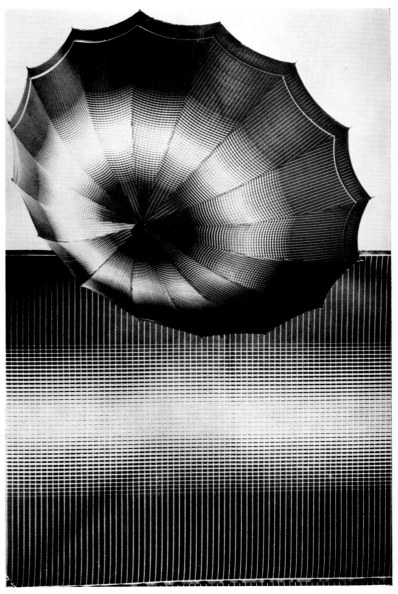

FIG. 47. FROM J. ADENSAMER & CIE., WIEN

FIG. 48. FROM A. FLEMMICH'S SÖHNE, WIEN

FIG. 49. FROM A. FLEMMICH'S SÖHNE, WIEN

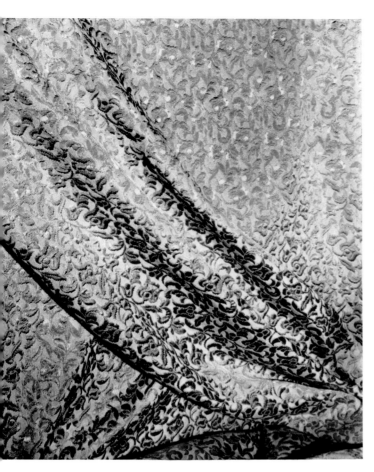

FIG. 50. FROM GEBRÜDER SCHIEL A.G., WIEN

FIG. 51. FROM GEBRÜDER SCHIEL A.G., WIEN

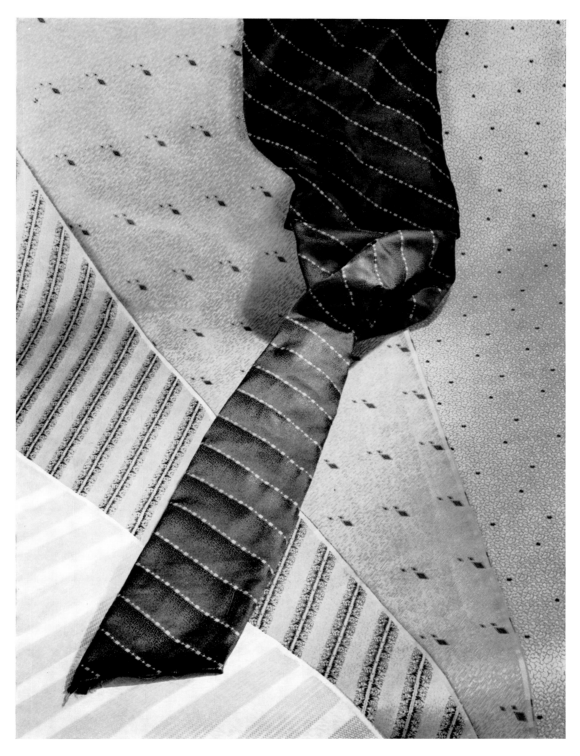

FIG. 52. FROM WIENER SEIDENWEBEREI ALFRED FIALA, WIEN

FIG. 53. FROM WIENER SEIDENWEBEREI ALFRED FIALA, WIEN

FIG. 54. FROM WIENER NEUSTÄDTER SEIDENINDUSTRIE KOBER & CO. K.G., WIEN

FIG. 55. FROM WIENER NEUSTÄDTER SEIDENINDUSTRIE KOBER & CO. K.G., WIEN

FIG. 56. FROM HEINRICH LÖRI, WIEN

FIG. 57. FROM HEINRICH LÖRI, WIEN

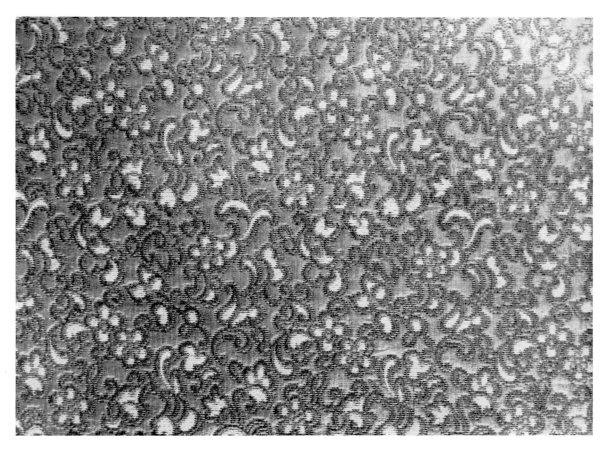

FIG. 58. FROM BRÜDER STEINER K.G., WIEN

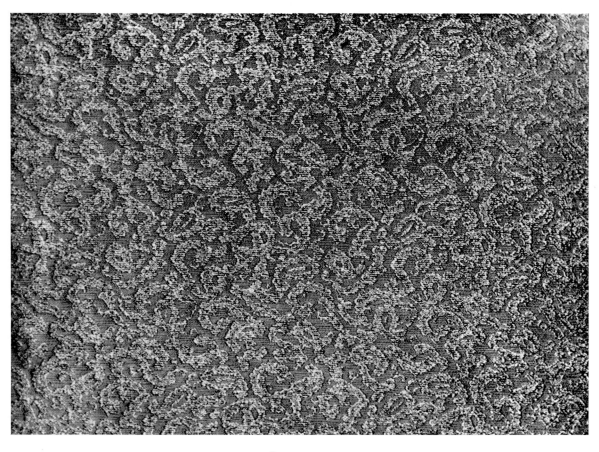

FIG. 59. FROM BRÜDER STEINER K.G., WIEN

FIG. 60. FROM BRÜDER STEINER K.G., WIEN

FIG. 61. FROM M. FABER & CO. K.G., WIEN

FIG. 62. FROM M. FABER & CO. K.G., WIEN

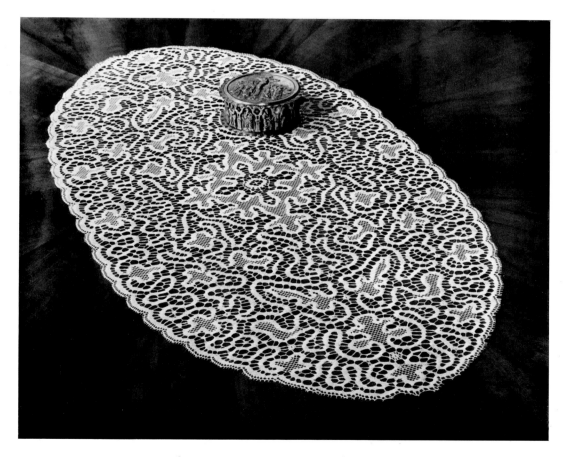

FIG. 63. FROM M. FABER & CO. K.G., WIEN

FIG. 64. FROM M. FABER & CO. K.G., WIEN

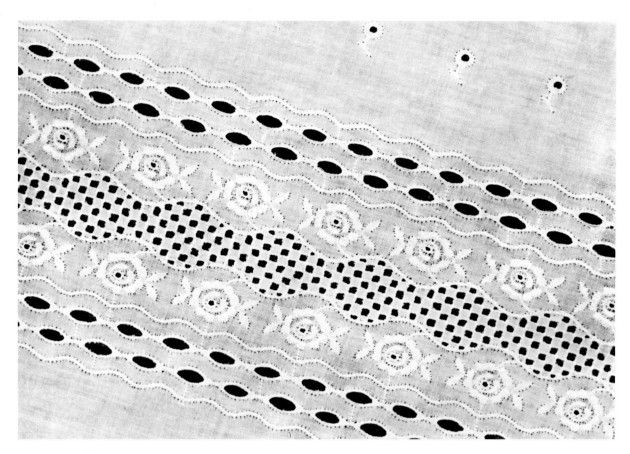

FIG. 65. FROM VERBAND DER VORARLBERGER STICKEREI-INDUSTRIE, DORNBIRN

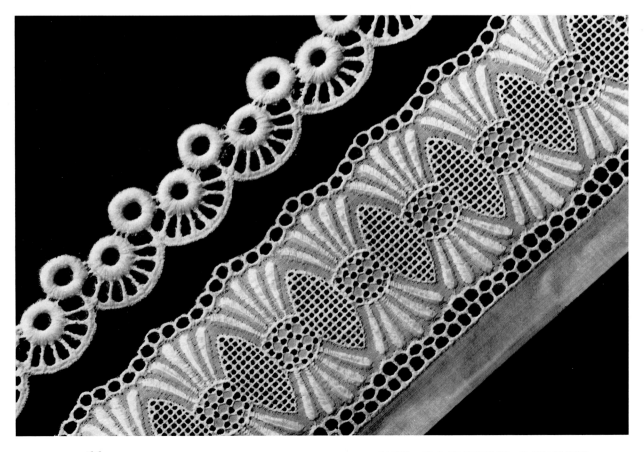

FIG. 66. FROM VERBAND DER VORARLBERGER STICKEREI-INDUSTRIE, DORNBIRN

FIG. 67. FROM VERBAND DER VORARLBERGER STICKEREI-
INDUSTRIE, DORNBIRN

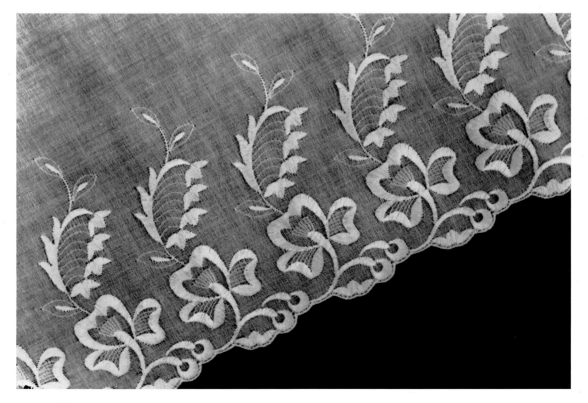

FIG. 68. FROM VERBAND DER VORARLBERGER STICKEREI-INDUSTRIE, DORNBIRN

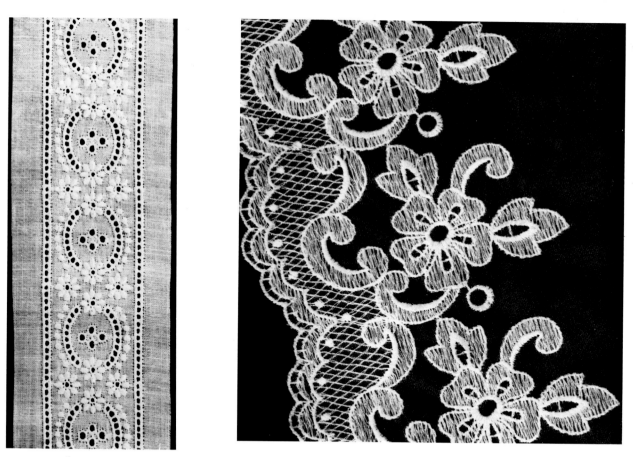

FIG. 69 & 70. FROM VERBAND DER VORARLBERGER STICKEREI-INDUSTRIE, DORNBIRN

FIG. 71. FROM VERBAND DER VORARLBERGER STICKEREI-INDUSTRIE, DORNBIRN

FIG. 72. FROM VERBAND DER VORARLBERGER STICKEREI-INDUSTRIE, DORNBIRN

FIG. 73. FROM VERBAND DER VORARLBERGER STICKEREI-INDUSTRIE, DORNBIRN

FIG. 74. FROM JERLAINE BENGER & CO., WIEN

FIG. 75. FROM JERLAINE BENGER & CO., WIEN

FIG. 76. FROM P. M. GLASER, WIEN

FIG. 77. FROM DOBYHAL & CO., WIEN

FIG. 78. FROM SIEGFRIED ELIAS, WIEN

FIG. 79. FROM 'HUMMER' WIENER MODE, WIEN

FIG. 80 & 81. FROM 'HUMMER' WIENER MODE, WIEN

FIG. 82 & 83 FROM MADELAINE FRANZ MÄSER, DORNBIRN

FIG. 84. FROM 'WISPO' PSCHIKAL & CO., WIEN

FIG. 85. FROM 'WISPO' PSCHIKAL & CO., WIEN

FIG. 87. FROM FRANZ KUGLER, WIEN

FIG. 86. FROM 'WISPO' PSCHIKAL & CO., WIEN

FIG. 88. FROM 'SPORT NOUVELLE' S. KATZ & CO.
K.G., WIEN

FIG. 89. FROM 'SPORT NOUVELLE' S. KATZ & CO. K.G., WIEN

FIG. 90. FROM BENEDIKT MÄSER, DORNBIRN

FIG. 91. FROM STEFFI ZAMBRA, WIEN

FIG. 92. FROM STEFFI ZAMBRA, WIEN

FIG. 93. FROM STEFFI ZAMBRA, WIEN

FIG. 95. FROM 'CORONA VIENNA' GÜNTHER TASSUL &
CO., WIEN

FIG. 94. FROM 'CORONA VIENNA' GÜNTHER TASSUL &
CO., WIEN

FIG. 96, 97 & 98 FROM LEOPOLD HOFFMANN, WIEN

FIG. 99. FROM 'HELLAS', JIRGENS & CO., WIEN